To

Colletta
_____

From

love from Beth
_____

Date

May 1, 2018
_____

Ellie Claire™ Gift & Paper Expressions
Brentwood, TN 37027
EllieClaire.com

It Is Well with My Soul
Promises of Comfort and Hope
A *Pocket Inspirations* Book
© 2013 by Ellie Claire, an imprint of Worthy Media, Inc.

ISBN 978-1-60936-867-8

Scripture quotations are taken from the following sources: The Holy Bible, King James Version (KJV). The Holy Bible, New International Version®, NIV®. Copyright © 1973, 1978, 1984, 2011 by Biblica, Inc.® All rights reserved worldwide. The Holy Bible, New King James Version® (NKJV). Copyright © 1982 by Thomas Nelson, Inc. The New American Standard Bible® (NASB), copyright © 1960, 1962, 1963, 1968, 1971, 1972, 1973, 1975, 1977, 1995 by The Lockman Foundation. The Holy Bible, New Living Translation (NLT), copyright 1996, 2004, 2007 by Tyndale House Foundation. Used by permission of Tyndale House Publishers, Inc., Carol Stream, Illinois 60188. *The Message* (MSG). Copyright © 1993, 1994, 1995, 1996, 2000, 2001, 2002. Used by permission of NavPress Publishing Group. *The Living Bible* (TLB) copyright © 1971 by Tyndale House Foundation. Used by permission of Tyndale House Publishers, Inc., Carol Stream, Illinois 60188. Used by permission. All rights reserved.

Excluding Scripture verses and deity pronouns, in some quotations references to men and masculine pronouns have been replaced with gender-neutral or feminine references. Additionally, in some quotations we have carefully updated verb forms and wording that may distract modern readers.

Stock or custom editions of Ellie Claire titles may be purchased in bulk for educational, business, ministry, fundraising, or sales promotional use. For information, please e-mail info@EllieClaire.com

Compiled by Barbara Farmer
Cover and interior design by Gearbox | studiogearbox.com

Printed in China

1 2 3 4 5 6 7 8 9 – 18 17 16 15 14 13

It Is Well with My Soul

PROMISES OF COMFORT & HOPE

Pi Pocket
INSPIRATIONS

Ellie
Claire
gift & paper expressions

inspired by life
EllieClaire.com

CONTENTS

Peace Like a River 6

Our Source of Strength............ 8

God's Compassion................. 10

Contemplating God 12

True Contentment................. 14

Precious Tears 16

Trust God's Heart................. 18

Showers of Blessings.............. 20

Grace for Trials..................... 22

Light in the Darkness............. 24

Sweet Comfort...................... 26

Intercession 28

Beauty of God's Peace 30

Seek the Lord 32

Every Need 34

Experience Peace 36

Unconditional...................... 38

Life of Faith 40

Hope in God........................ 42

Settled in Solitude 44

God Understands 46

Sought and Found 48

New Every Morning 50

Faithful Guide 52

My Help.............................. 54

Sweet Hour of Prayer............. 56

Fresh Hope 58

God Listens 60

Just the Beginning 62

Totally Aware....................... 64

God's Answers 66

Take Refuge 68

To Know Him 70

The Weaver 72

Comforted by God................. 74

In the Silence 76

Treasure in Nature................. 78

Forever Grateful.................... 80

God's Guidance 82

Renewed Strength................. 84

The Goodness of God............. 86

Place of Rest........................ 88

Powerful Love 90

Mighty to Keep 92

Overcoming......................... 94

Seek First 96

Steps of Faith....................... 98

Shining Promises 100

Delight in the Lord 102

Countless Beauties............... 104

Your Personal God 106

Waiting Quietly................... 108

Pour Out Your Heart 110

Always There 112

Rest in Him 114

An Invitation...................... 116

River of Delights 118

A Safe Journey.................... 120

Made for Joy 122

The Gift of Grace 124

God's Eternal Love 126

Peace Like a River

When peace, like a river, attendeth my way,
When sorrows like sea billows roll;
Whatever my lot, Thou hast taught me to say,
It is well, it is well, with my soul.

The Lord is my shepherd; I shall not want.
He makes me to lie down in green pastures;
He leads me beside the still waters.
He restores my soul.

PSALM 23:1–3 NKJV

I will let God's peace infuse every part of today. As
the chaos swirls and life's demands pull at me on all
sides, I will breathe in God's peace that surpasses all
understanding. He has promised that He would set
within me a peace too deeply planted to be affected by
unexpected or exhausting demands.

Calm me, O Lord, as You stilled the storm,
Still me, O Lord, keep me from harm.
Let all the tumult within me cease,
Enfold me, Lord, in Your peace.

CELTIC TRADITIONAL

Only Christ Himself, who slept in the boat in the
storm and then spoke calm to the wind and waves, can
stand beside us when we are in a panic and say to us
Peace. It will not be explainable. It transcends human
understanding. And there is nothing else like it
in the whole wide world.

ELISABETH ELLIOT

*How much greater is my peace when I find it has
come in the midst of the storm and not because
He stilled its forces.*

LEITA TWYEFFORT

Our Source of Strength

We must drink deeply from the very Source the deep calm
and peace of interior quietude and refreshment of God,
allowing the pure water of divine grace to flow plentifully
and unceasingly from the Source itself.

MOTHER TERESA

*Jesus stood and said… "Let anyone who is thirsty come to me and
drink. Whoever believes in me, as Scripture has said, rivers of
living water will flow from within them."*

JOHN 7:37–38 NIV

He is the Source. Of everything. Strength for your day.
Wisdom for your task. Comfort for your soul. Grace for
your battle. Provision for each need. Understanding for
each failure. Assistance for every encounter.

JACK HAYFORD

*We take our lead from Christ,
who is the source of everything we do.*

EPHESIANS 4:16 MSG

Grasp the fact that God is for you—let this certainty make
its impact on you in relation to what you are up against
at this very moment; and you will find in thus knowing
God as your sovereign protector, irrevocably committed
to you in the covenant of grace, both freedom from fear
and new strength for the fight.

J. I. Packer

We have a Father in heaven who is almighty, who loves His
children as He loves His only-begotten Son, and whose
very joy and delight it is to…help them at all times and
under all circumstances.

George Müeller

*Trust is giving up what little I have in strength
and power so I can confidently relax in His
power and strength.*

Gloria Gaither

God's Compassion

This I recall to my mind,
Therefore I have hope.
The LORD's lovingkindnesses indeed never cease,
For His compassions never fail.
They are new every morning;
Great is Your faithfulness.
"The LORD is my portion," says my soul,
"Therefore I have hope in Him."
The LORD is good to those who wait for Him,
To the person who seeks Him.

LAMENTATIONS 3:21—25 NASB

The loving God we serve has immeasurable compassion
and tenderness toward each of us throughout our lives.

DR. JAMES DOBSON

Only God can heal the sorrow you feel. His gifts of
peace, comfort, and compassion may feel elusive at
times. But remember, feelings don't paint an accurate
picture of the truth. Keep reaching out to Him, even
when tears are all you have to offer.

God is as near as a whispered prayer
No matter the time or place,
Whether skies are blue
And all's right with you,
Or clouds dim the road you face.
In His mercy and great compassion
He will ease, He will help, He will share!
Whatever your lot,
Take heart in the thought:
God's as near as a whispered prayer!

JON GILBERT

Grace is…an outpouring, a boundless…offering of God's self to us, suffering with us, overflowing with tenderness. Grace is God's passion.

DR. GERALD G. MAY

You, O Lord, are a God full of compassion,
and gracious, longsuffering
and abundant in mercy and truth.

PSALM 86:15 NKJV

Contemplating God

We are so preciously loved by God that we cannot even
comprehend it. No created being can ever know how
much and how sweetly and tenderly God loves them.
It is only with the help of His grace that we are able to
persevere in spiritual contemplation with endless wonder
at His high, surpassing, immeasurable love which our
Lord in His goodness has for us.

JULIAN OF NORWICH

Take a moment to consider the awesome reality that the
God who spoke and created the universe is now speaking
to you. If Jesus could speak and raise the dead, calm a
storm…and heal the incurable, then what effect might a
word from Him have upon your life?

HENRY T. BLACKABY

Contemplation is nothing else but a secret, peaceful, and
loving infusion of God, which, if admitted, will set the
soul on fire with the spirit of love.

JOHN OF THE CROSS

LORD, our Lord,
how majestic is your name in all the earth!…
When I consider your heavens,
the work of your fingers,
the moon and the stars,
which you have set in place,
what is mankind that you are mindful of them,
human beings that you care for them?
You have made them a little lower than the angels
and crowned them with glory and honor.

PSALM 8:1, 3–5 NIV

*Night by night I will lie down
and sleep in the thought of God.*
WILLIAM MOUNTFORD

True Contentment

True contentment is a real, even an active, virtue—not
only affirmative but creative. It is the power of getting
out of any situation all there is in it.

G. K. CHESTERTON

As God helps you see more clearly what really matters
in this world, contentment spreads its sense of peaceful
appreciation deeper into your soul. That hunger to strive
for more is replaced by a hunger to know more of God.
That's what lies at the heart of living a full life.

Do you want to stand out? Then step down. Be a servant.
If you puff yourself up, you'll get the wind knocked out of you.
But if you're content to simply be yourself,
your life will count for plenty.

MATTHEW 23:11–12 MSG

Today I give it all to Jesus…my hopes, my plans
and dreams and schemes, my fears and failures—all.
Peace and contentment come when the struggle ceases.

GLORIA GAITHER

Becoming content with your life isn't an impossible goal
to strive for; it's a reality that's available to you now.
Gratitude for what God has already given you
is an essential element in learning to be content.
Thank God for His provision, and rest in the knowledge
that He will continue to provide.

*I know what it is to be in need, and I know what it is
to have plenty. I have learned the secret of being
content in any and every situation.*

PHILIPPIANS 4:12 NIV

*Where the soul is full of peace and joy, outward
surroundings and circumstances are of
comparatively little account.*

HANNAH WHITALL SMITH

Precious Tears

There is a sacredness in tears.
They are not the mark of weakness, but of power.
They speak more eloquently than ten thousand tongues.
They are the messengers of overwhelming grief,
of deep contrition, and of unspeakable love.

WASHINGTON IRVING

Your tears are precious to God. They are like
stained-glass windows in the darkness, whose true beauty
is revealed only when there is a light within.

We can be assured of this: God, who knows all
and sees all, will set all things straight in the end.
Even better, He will dry every tear.

RICHARD J. FOSTER

A teardrop on earth
summons the King of Heaven.

CHARLES R. SWINDOLL

The sun will no more be your light by day,
nor will the brightness of the moon shine on you,
for the LORD will be your everlasting light,
and your God will be your glory.
Your sun will never set again,
and your moon will wane no more;
the LORD will be your everlasting light,
and your days of sorrow will end.

God comforts. He doesn't pity. He picks us up,
dries our tears, soothes our fears,
and lifts our thoughts beyond the hurt.

DR. ROBERT SCHULLER

You keep track of all my sorrows.
You have collected all my tears in your bottle.
You have recorded each one in your book.

PSALM 56:8 NLT

Trust God's Heart

Knowing God is putting your trust in Him.
Trust that He loves you and will provide for your every
need. When we know God, we know Him like a personal
friend. We have no reason to be scared of God.
God is for us! He will never leave us. Having "fear"
of the Lord is the same as having "deepest respect."
Because of who He is we have every reason to feel respect
for Him and show it in the way that we live.
We no longer fear the unknown, fear the future,
or fear our circumstances.

TOM RICHARDS

Trust in the LORD with all your heart;
do not depend on your own understanding.
Seek his will in all you do,
and he will show you which path to take.

PROVERBS 3:5—6 NLT

He wants you to sense His presence. He wants you
to trust that when you are afraid, you can turn to Him
and find His peace. When you are weary, you will find
His strength.... And when you are in the middle of
a raging storm, you will find His shelter and provision.

STORMIE OMARTIAN

In those times I can't seem to find God,
I rest in the assurance He knows how to find me.

NEVA COYLE

Be content with what you have,
because God has said, "Never will I leave you;
never will I forsake you."

HEBREWS 13:5 NIV

Showers of Blessings

God, who is love—who is, if I may say it this way,
made out of love—simply cannot help but shed
blessing on blessing upon us.

HANNAH WHITALL SMITH

Bless the LORD, O my soul;
And all that is within me, bless His holy name!
Bless the LORD, O my soul,
And forget not all His benefits:
Who forgives all your iniquities,
Who heals all your diseases,
Who redeems your life from destruction,
Who crowns you with lovingkindness and tender mercies,
Who satisfies your mouth with good things,
So that your youth is renewed like the eagle's.

PSALM 103:1–5 NKJV

Lift up your eyes. Your heavenly Father waits to bless
you—in inconceivable ways to make your life what you
never dreamed it could be.

ANNE ORTLUND

God is waiting for us to come to Him with our needs.... God's throne room is always open.... Every single believer in the whole world could walk into the throne room all at one time, and it would not even be crowded.

CHARLES STANLEY

Wind, rain, falling leaves of autumn,
Winter snow, springing flow'rs, and the sun shine
Forth the light of Your love; countless blessings from above,
As from season to season in You we live and move—
Moved to praise You alway
For the brightness You pour on our way.

JACK HAYFORD

I will send the showers they need.
There will be showers of blessings.

EZEKIEL 34:26 NLT

Grace for Trials

God has not promised skies always blue,
flower-strewn pathways all our lives through;
God has not promised sun without rain,
joy without sorrow, peace without pain.
But God has promised strength for the day,
rest for the labor, light for the way,
grace for the trials, help from above,
unfailing sympathy, undying love.

ANNIE JOHNSON FLINT

I know the LORD is always with me.
I will not be shaken, for he is right beside me.
No wonder my heart is glad, and I rejoice.
My body rests in safety.

PSALM 16:8—9 NLT

Character cannot be developed in ease and quiet.
Only through experience of trial
and suffering can the soul be strengthened.

HELEN KELLER

We also rejoice in our sufferings, because we know
that suffering produces perseverance; perseverance,
character; and character, hope. And hope does not
disappoint us, because God has poured out his love into
our hearts by the Holy Spirit, whom he has given us.

ROMANS 5:3–5 NIV

This is peace—to be able to sleep in the storm!
In Christ, we are relaxed and at peace in the midst
of the confusions...and perplexities of this life.
The storm rages, but our hearts are at rest.

BILLY GRAHAM

After winter comes the summer.
After night comes the dawn. And after every
storm, there comes clear, open skies.

SAMUEL RUTHERFORD

Light in the Darkness

There is not enough darkness in all the world to put
out the light of one small candle.... In moments of
discouragement, defeat, or even despair, there are
always certain things to cling to. Little things usually:
remembered laughter, the face of a sleeping child,
a tree in the wind—in fact, any reminder of something
deeply felt or dearly loved. No one is so poor as not to
have many of these small candles. When they are lighted,
darkness goes away and a touch of wonder remains.

ARTHUR GORDON

Your word is a lamp to my feet
And a light to my path.

PSALM 119:105 NKJV

I believe that God is in me as the sun is in the color
and fragrance of a flower—the Light in my darkness,
the Voice in my silence.

HELEN KELLER

It should fill us with joy, that infinite wisdom guides
the affairs of the world…that infinite wisdom directs
every event, brings order out of confusion, and light
out of darkness, and, to those who love God, causes
all things, whatever be their present aspect and apparent
tendency, to work together for good.

J. L. DAGG

One taper lights a thousand,
Yet shines as it has shone;
And the humblest light may kindle
One brighter than its own.

HEZEKIAH BUTTERWORTH

You light a lamp for me.
The LORD, my God,
lights up my darkness.

PSALM 18:28 NLT

Sweet Comfort

God comforts. He lays His right hand
on the wounded soul…and He says,
as if that one were the only soul in all the universe:
O greatly beloved, fear not: peace be unto thee.

AMY CARMICHAEL

There is a place of comfort sweet
Near to the heart of God,
A place where we our Savior meet,
Near to the heart of God.
O Jesus, blest Redeemer,
Sent from the heart of God,
Hold us who wait before Thee
Near to the heart of God.

CLELAND B. MCAFEE

We may ask, "Why does God bring thunderclouds
and disasters when we want green pastures and still
waters?" Bit by bit, we find behind the clouds,
the Father's feet; behind the lightning, an abiding day
that has no night; behind the thunder, a still small voice
that comforts with a comfort that is unspeakable.

OSWALD CHAMBERS

The LORD is near to the brokenhearted
And saves those who are crushed in spirit.

PSALM 34:18 NASB

Peace *with* God brings the peace *of* God. It is a peace
that settles our nerves, fills our mind, floods our spirit,
and in the midst of the uproar around us, gives us the
assurance that everything is all right.

BOB MUMFORD

He walks with me, and he talks with me,
and he tells me I am his own.
And the joy we share as we tarry there
none other has ever known.

C. AUSTIN MILES

*It is such a comfort to drop the tangles of life
into God's hands and leave them there.*

L. B. COWMAN

Intercession

*The Holy Spirit helps us in our weakness. For example,
we don't know what God wants us to pray for. But the Holy Spirit
prays for us with groanings that cannot be expressed in words.
And the Father who knows all hearts knows what the Spirit
is saying, for the Spirit pleads for us believers in harmony
with God's own will. And we know that God causes everything
to work together for the good of those who love God
and are called according to his purpose for them.*

ROMANS 8:26–28 NLT

We can make our lives a prayer by becoming aware
of God in each moment as we move through our day,
whether we're having a breathtaking moment
of adventure and beauty or performing a mundane task.
God is the God of the present;
he is each moment and he wants to be found.

MIA POHLMAN

When life tumbles in, problems overwhelm us,
and our prayers reach out beyond our limited
vocabulary, how reassuring it is to know that the Spirit
makes intercession for us!

HAZEL C. LEE

Prayer is such an ordinary, everyday, mundane thing.
Certainly, people who pray...are people
who want to share a life with God,
to love and be loved, to speak and to listen,
to work and to be at rest in the presence of God.

ROBERTA BONDI

*If you don't know what you're doing,
pray to the Father. He loves to help.*

JAMES 1:5 MSG

Beauty of God's Peace

Let not your heart be troubled; you believe in God, believe also in Me. In My Father's house are many mansions; if it were not so, I would have told you. I go to prepare a place for you. And if I go and prepare a place for you, I will come again, and receive you to Myself; that where I am, there you may be also.... I will not leave you orphans: I will come to you.... Peace I leave with you, My peace I give to you; not as the world gives do I give to you. Let not your heart be troubled, neither let it be afraid.

JOHN 14:1–3, 18, 27 NKJV

The peace of God is that eternal calm
which lies far too deep down to be reached
by any external trouble or disturbance.

ARTHUR T. PIERSON

If peace be in the heart, the wildest winter storm
is full of solemn beauty.

C. F. RICHARDSON

Drop Thy still dews of quietness
till all our strivings cease;
take from our souls the strain and stress,
and let our ordered lives confess
the beauty of Thy peace.

JOHN GREENLEAF WHITTIER

May the God of love and peace set your heart at rest
and speed you on your journey.

RAYMOND OF PENYAFORT

*I listen carefully to what God
the LORD is saying, for he
speaks peace to his faithful people.*

PSALM 85:8 NLT

Seek the Lord

In extravagance of soul we seek His face.
In generosity of heart, we glean His gentle touch.
In excessiveness of spirit, we love Him and His love
comes back to us a hundredfold.

TRICIA McCARY RHODES

*The God who made the world and everything in it
is the Lord of heaven and earth.... He himself gives all men life
and breath and everything else.... God did this so that men
would seek him and perhaps reach out for him and find him,
though he is not far from each one of us.
"For in him we live, and move, and have our being."*

ACTS 17:24–25, 27–28 NIV

I have sought Your nearness;
With all my heart have I called You,
And going out to meet You
I found You coming toward me.

YEHUDA HALEVI

32

One thing I ask of the LORD,
this is what I seek:
that I may dwell in the house of the LORD
all the days of my life,
to gaze upon the beauty of the LORD
and to seek him in his temple.

PSALM 27:4 NIV

God is not an elusive dream or a phantom to chase,
but a divine person to know.
He does not avoid us, but seeks us.
When we seek Him, the contact is instantaneous.

NEVA COYLE

I love those who love me;
and those who diligently seek me
will find me.

PROVERBS 8:17 NASB

33

Every Need

"So do not fear, for I am with you;
do not be dismayed, for I am your God.
I will strengthen you and help you;
I will uphold you with my righteous right hand....
For I am the LORD, your God,
who takes hold of your right hand
and says to you, do not fear....
for I myself will help you," declares the LORD....
I will make rivers flow on barren heights,
and springs within the valleys.
I will turn the desert into pools of water,
and the parched ground into springs.

ISAIAH 41:10, 13–14, 18 NIV

God wants nothing from us except our needs,
and these furnish Him with room to display
His bounty when He supplies them freely.... Not what
I have, but what I do not have, is the first point
of contact between my soul and God.

CHARLES H. SPURGEON

34

Jesus Christ has brought every need, every joy,
every gratitude, every hope of ours before God. He
accompanies us and brings us into the presence of God.

DIETRICH BONHOEFFER

Live today! Live fully each moment of today. Trust God
to let you work through this moment and the next.
He will give you all you need. Don't skip over
the painful or confusing moment—even it has its important
and rightful place in the day.

*My God is changeless in his love for me
and he will come and help me.*

PSALM 59:10 TLB

Experience Peace

Trials…may come in abundance. But they cannot
penetrate into the sanctuary of the soul when it is settled
in God, and we may dwell in perfect peace.

HANNAH WHITALL SMITH

When disappointment leaves you discouraged,
remember God has something better in mind.
Trade your heartache for anticipation as you wait
for the beauty of God's plan to unfold.

*We've been surrounded and battered by troubles, but we're not
demoralized; we're not sure what to do, but we know that God
knows what to do;…we've been thrown down, but we haven't
broken. What they did to Jesus, they do to us…; what Jesus did
among them, he does in us—he lives!*

2 CORINTHIANS 4:8—10 MSG

Peace is a margin of power around our daily need.
Peace is a consciousness of springs too deep
for earthly droughts to dry up.

HARRY EMERSON FOSDICK

36

Unceasing prayer has a way of speaking peace
to the chaos. Our fractured and fragmented activities
begin focusing around a new Center of Reference.
We experience peace, stillness, serenity,
firmness of life orientation.

RICHARD J. FOSTER

I believe in the sun even when it is not shining.
I believe in love even when I do not feel it.
I believe in God even when He is silent.

Only God gives true peace—a quiet gift He sets within us
just when we think we've exhausted our search for it.

He calmed the storm to a whisper
and stilled the waves.
What a blessing was that stillness.

PSALM 107:29—30 NLT

Unconditional

In His love of us and for us God freely wills not to be
without us and wills to be with us as those whom He has
eternally chosen to coexist with Himself and share His
eternal love. In His super-abounding and overflowing
love He does not want to be alone without us or want us
to be alone without him...there is and can be no other
God than this God whose very Being is the One
who loves us and will not be without us.

THOMAS TORRANCE

Do you believe that the God of Jesus loves you beyond
worthiness and unworthiness, beyond fidelity
and infidelity; that he loves you in the morning sun
and the evening rain; that he loves you when your
intellect denies it, your emotions refuse it, your whole
being rejects it? Do you believe that God loves without
condition or reservation, and loves you this moment
as you are and not as you should be?

BRENNAN MANNING

Though the mountains be shaken
and the hills be removed,
yet my unfailing love for you will not be shaken.

ISAIAH 54:10 NIV

Nothing we can do will make the Father love us less;
nothing we do can make Him love us more.
He loves us unconditionally with an everlasting love.

NANCIE CARMICHAEL

See what great love the Father has lavished
on us, that we should be called children of God!
And that is what we are!

1 JOHN 3:1 NIV

Life of Faith

Our Heavenly Father…wants us to reach up and take His
hand, but He doesn't want us to *ever* let go. In fact, His
desire is that we become *more* and *more* dependent upon
Him for every step. That's because He wants to take
us to places we've never been. To heights we can't even
imagine…. God always requires the first step to be ours.
In order to take that first step, we must look into the
face of God, reach up and take His hand, and say,
"Lead me in the path You have for me, Lord.
From this day on I want to walk with You."

STORMIE OMARTIAN

God can do anything, you know—far more than
you could ever imagine or guess or request in your wildest dreams!
He does it…by working within us,
his Spirit deeply and gently within us.

EPHESIANS 3:20—21 MSG

Living a life of faith means never knowing where you
are being led. But it does mean loving and knowing
the One who is leading. It is literally a life of faith,
not of understanding and reason—
a life of knowing Him who calls us to go.

OSWALD CHAMBERS

Faith is to believe what we do not see;
and the reward of this faith is to see what we believe.

AUGUSTINE

For we walk by faith, not by sight.

2 CORINTHIANS 5:7 NKJV

Hope in God

When you accept the fact that sometimes seasons are dry
and times are hard and that God is in control of both,
you will discover a sense of divine refuge, because the
hope then is in God and not in yourself.

CHARLES R. SWINDOLL

Why are you cast down, O my soul?
And why are you disquieted within me?
Hope in God, for I shall yet praise Him
For the help of His countenance.
O my God, my soul is cast down within me;
Therefore I will remember You....
Deep calls unto deep at the noise of Your waterfalls;
All Your waves and billows have gone over me.
The LORD will command His lovingkindness in the daytime,
And in the night His song shall be with me—
A prayer to the God of my life.

PSALM 42:5–8 NKJV

Life is what we are alive to. It is not length but breadth....
Be alive to...goodness, kindness, purity, love, history,
poetry, music, flowers, stars, God, and eternal hope.

MALTBIE D. BABCOCK

You are never alone. In your heart of hearts, in the place
where no two people are ever alike, Christ is waiting for
you. And what you never dared hope for springs to life.

ROGER OF TAIZÉ

Hope is faith holding out its hands in the dark.

GEORGE ILES

*We put our hope in the LORD.
He is our help and our shield.
In him our hearts rejoice,
for we trust in his holy name.*

PSALM 33:20–21 NLT

Settled in Solitude

Solitude liberates us from entanglements by carving out
a space from which we can see ourselves and our situation
before the Audience of One. Solitude provides the
private place where we can take our bearings
and so make God our North Star.

OS GUINNESS

Over the margins of life comes a whisper,
a faint call, a premonition of richer living which we
know we are passing by. Strained by the very mad pace
of our daily outer burdens, we are further strained
by an inward uneasiness, because we have hints
that there is a way of life vastly richer and deeper
than all this hurried existence,
a life of unhurried serenity and peace and power.

THOMAS R. KELLY

What happens when we live God's way? He brings gifts into
our lives, much the same way that fruit appears in an orchard—
things like affection for others, exuberance about life, serenity.

GALATIANS 5:22 MSG

Don't ever let yourself get so busy that you miss those
little but important extras in life—the beauty of a day...
the smile of a friend...the serenity of a quiet moment
alone. For it is often life's smallest pleasures and gentlest
joys that make the biggest and most lasting difference.

Settle yourself in solitude and you will
come upon Him in yourself.

TERESA OF ÀVILA

You're my place of quiet retreat;
I wait for your Word to renew me.

PSALM 119:114 MSG

God Understands

Your heavenly Father is reaching for your hand.
He knows you work hard. He knows you give your
all but sometimes come up short. He knows when
you're worn out by life and feel faint in your faith.
God understands when you feel like crawling into
a hole or plopping down in defeat. When you feel like
you've endured one too many losses, God wants you
to simply put your hand in His—and trust. He promises
to exchange His strength for your weariness.

He heals the brokenhearted
and binds up their wounds.
He determines the number of the stars
and calls them each by name.
Great is our Lord and mighty in power;
his understanding has no limit....
The LORD delights in those who fear him,
who put their hope in his unfailing love.

PSALM 147:3–5, 11 NIV

You can talk to God because God listens. Your voice matters in heaven. He takes you very seriously.... No need to fear that you will be ignored. Even if you stammer or stumble, even if what you have to say impresses no one, it impresses God—and He listens.

MAX LUCADO

God possesses infinite knowledge and an awareness which is uniquely His. At all times, even in the midst of any type of suffering, I can realize that He knows, loves, watches, understands, and more than that, He has a purpose.

BILLY GRAHAM

God understands our prayers even when we can't find the words to say them.

Sought and Found

God's holy beauty comes near you, like a spiritual scent,
and it stirs your drowsing soul…. He creates in you
the desire to find Him and run after Him—to follow
wherever He leads you, and to press peacefully against
His heart wherever He is.

JOHN OF THE CROSS

You will call on me and come and pray to me,
and I will listen to you. You will seek me and find me
when you seek me with all your heart.

JEREMIAH 29:12–13 NIV

It is God's will that we believe that we see Him
continually, though it seems to us that the sight
be only partial; and through this belief He makes us
always to gain more grace, for God wishes to be seen,
and He wishes to be sought, and He wishes
to be expected, and He wishes to be trusted.

JULIAN OF NORWICH

God can be and wants to be found in everything we do.
In every moment of life, God is waiting to reveal himself
to us and fulfill us through the revelation of who he is.

MIA POHLMAN

They who seek the throne of grace
Find that throne in every place;
If we live a life of prayer,
God is present everywhere.

OLIVER HOLDEN

To seek God means first of all to let yourself
be found by Him.

Seek the LORD your God,
and you will find Him if you search for Him
with all your heart and all your soul.

DEUTERONOMY 4:29 NASB

49

New Every Morning

Experience God in the breathless wonder and startling
beauty that is all around you. His sun shines warm upon
your face. His wind whispers in the treetops.
Like the first rays of morning light,
celebrate the start of each day with God.

WENDY MOORE

Satisfy us in the morning with your unfailing love,
that we may sing for joy and be glad all our days.

PSALM 90:14 NIV

The sun...in its full glory, either at rising or setting—
this, and many other like blessings we enjoy daily;
and for the most of them, because they are so common,
most men forget to pay their praises.
But let not us.

IZAAK WALTON

Life begins each morning.... Each morning is the open
door to a new world—new vistas, new aims, new tryings.

LEIGH MITCHELL HODGES

Grace comes into the soul as the morning sun
into the world; first a dawning, then a light;
and at last the sun in his full and excellent brightness.

THOMAS ADAMS

A quiet morning with a loving God puts the events
of the upcoming day into proper perspective.

JANETTE OKE

In the morning let our hearts gaze upon God's love
and the love He has allowed us to share, and in the beauty
of that vision, let us go forth to meet the day.

ROY LESSIN

*Always new. Always exciting.
Always full of promise. The mornings of our
lives, each a personal daily miracle!*

GLORIA GAITHER

Faithful Guide

Guidance is a sovereign act. Not merely does God will
to guide us by showing us His way;…whatever mistakes
we may make, we shall come safely home. Slippings and
strayings there will be, no doubt, but the everlasting arms
are beneath us; we shall be caught, rescued, restored.
This is God's promise; this is how good He is. And our
self-distrust, while keeping us humble, must not cloud
the joy with which we lean on our faithful covenant God.

J. I. PACKER

Heaven often seems distant and unknown,
but if he who made the road…is our guide,
we need not fear to lose the way.

HENRY VAN DYKE

*When we obey him, every path he guides us on is fragrant
with his loving-kindness and his truth.*

PSALM 25:10 TLB

We are of such value to God that He came to
live among us…and to guide us home.
He will go to any length to seek us, even to being lifted
high upon the cross to draw us back to Himself.
We can only respond by loving God for His love.

CATHERINE OF SIENNA

*Let us draw near to God with a sincere heart and with the full
assurance that faith brings.… Let us hold unswervingly
to the hope we profess, for he who promised is faithful.*

HEBREWS 10:22–23 NIV

*May God's love guide you through the special
plans He has for your life.*

My Help

I lift up my eyes to the hills—
where does my help come from?
My help comes from the LORD,
the Maker of heaven and earth.
He will not let your foot slip—
he who watches over you will not slumber;
indeed, he who watches over Israel
will neither slumber nor sleep.
The LORD watches over you—
the LORD is your shade at your right hand;
the sun will not harm you by day,
nor the moon by night.
The LORD will keep you from all harm—
he will watch over your life;
the LORD will watch over your coming and going
both now and forevermore.

PSALM 121:1–8 NIV

We may not all reach God's ideal for us,
but with His help we may move in that direction
day by day as we relate every detail of our lives to Him.

CAROL GISH

Be assured, if you walk with Him and look to Him
and expect help from Him, He will never fail you.

GEORGE MÜELLER

*Let us draw near with confidence to the throne of grace,
so that we may receive mercy and find grace to help in time of need.*

HEBREWS 4:16 NASB

Have courage for the great sorrows of life, and patience
for the small ones; and when you have…accomplished
your daily task, go to sleep in peace. God is awake.

VICTOR HUGO

*Trust the LORD!
He is your helper and your shield.*

PSALM 115:9 NLT

Sweet Hour of Prayer

Sweet hour of prayer, sweet hour of prayer,
That calls me from a world of care,
And bids me at my Father's throne,
Make all my wants and wishes known!
In seasons of distress and grief,
My soul has often found relief,
And oft escaped the tempter's snare
By Thy return, sweet hour of prayer.

WILLIAM W. WALFORD

If we knew how to listen, we would hear Him speaking
to us. For God does speak.... If we knew how to listen
to God, if we knew how to look around us,
our whole life would become prayer.

MICHAEL QUOIST

*I love the LORD because he hears my voice
and my prayer for mercy.
Because he bends down to listen,
I will pray as long as I have breath!*

PSALM 116:1–2 NLT

When you come into the presence of God,
He draws near to you to listen to what is on your heart.
Delighting in your presence, He hushes the heavenly host
to hear the petitions you bring. And pleased
with every indication of your increasing trust,
He receives your praise and gratitude,
responding in Spirit with peace and joy.

All good meditative prayer is a conversion
of our entire self to God.

THOMAS MERTON

*I call on you, O God, for you will answer me;
give ear to me and hear my prayer.*

PSALM 17:6 NIV

Fresh Hope

God specializes in things fresh and firsthand.
His plans for you this year may outshine those
of the past.... He's preparing to fill your days
with reasons to give Him praise.

JONI EARECKSON TADA

GOD...rekindles burned-out lives with fresh hope,
restoring dignity and respect to their lives—
a place in the sun!

1 SAMUEL 2:6–7 MSG

Whatever your years, there is in every
being's heart the love of wonder, the undaunted
challenges of events, the unfailing childlike appetite
for what comes next, and the joy of the game of life.
You are as young as your hope.

GENERAL DOUGLAS MACARTHUR

The hope we have is a living hope, an unassailable one.
We wait for it, in faith and patience.

ELISABETH ELLIOT

Authentic hope is the confidence that no matter what the outcome, God will see you through all of life's challenges and difficulties. That's not wishful thinking; that's a certainty. That requires a shift from insisting upon a particular way you think things should go to deciding that no matter how things go, God will be your constant companion and source of comfort.

Each dawn holds a new hope for a new plan, making the start of each day the start of a new life.

GINA BLAIR

Let your unfailing love surround us, LORD,
for our hope is in you alone.

PSALM 33:22 NLT

Within each of us, just waiting to blossom,
is the wonderful promise of all we can be.

God Listens

There will be times in life when nothing makes any sense.
We hoped for something great and came up empty.
But be assured that even in this place of darkness,
God is present. Throughout history, every great work
of God started in this exact place of emptiness.
God fills those things that are empty.

We come this morning—
Like empty pitchers to a full fountain,
With no merits of our own,
O Lord—open up a window of heaven…
And listen this morning.

JAMES WELDON JOHNSON

God listens in compassion and love,
just like we do when our children come to us.
He delights in our presence. When we do this,
we will discover something of inestimable value.
We will discover that by praying we learn to pray.

RICHARD J. FOSTER

You don't need a telescope, a microscope, or a horoscope
to realize the fullness of Christ, and the emptiness
of the universe without him. When you come to him,
that fullness comes together for you, too.

COLOSSIANS 2:7–9 MSG

God came to us because God wanted to join us
on the road, to listen to our story, and to help us realize
that we are not walking in circles but moving toward
the house of peace and joy.

HENRI J. M. NOUWEN

When we call on God, He bends down His ear
to listen, as a father bends down
to listen to his little child.

ELIZABETH CHARLES

Just the Beginning

We cannot believe that a writer is a terrible person
simply because the hero of the book goes through
terrible times. On the contrary, we believe that
a good author won't leave the hero in despair.
A good author will provide a way out.
In the same way, when we come to God with our burdens,
we must understand that the story isn't over. God is ready
to write the best possible ending to each person's life.

No test or temptation that comes your way is beyond
the course of what others have had to face.
All you need to remember is that God will never let you down…
he'll always be there to help you come through it.

1 CORINTHIANS 10:13 MSG

The Lord's goodness surrounds us at every moment.
I walk through it almost with difficulty,
as through thick grass and flowers.

R. W. BARBER

The LORD longs to be gracious to you;
he rises to show you compassion.
For the LORD is a God of justice.
Blessed are all who wait for him!

ISAIAH 30:18 NIV

God never abandons anyone on whom
He has set His love; nor does Christ,
the good shepherd, ever lose track of His sheep.

J. I. PACKER

Be strong and courageous! Do not be afraid...!
For the LORD your God will personally go ahead
of you. He will neither fail you nor abandon you.

DEUTERONOMY 31:6 NLT

Totally Aware

God is every moment totally aware of each one of us.
Totally aware in intense concentration and love.... No
one passes through any area of life, happy or tragic,
without the attention of God with him.

EUGENIA PRICE

Because God is responsible for our welfare, we are told
to cast all our care upon Him, for He cares for us.
God says, "I'll take the burden—don't give it a thought—
leave it to Me." God is keenly aware that we are
dependent upon Him for life's necessities.

BILLY GRAHAM

You are God's created beauty and the focus
of His affection and delight.

JANET L. WEAVER SMITH

*I am convinced that neither death nor life, neither angels nor
demons, neither the present nor the future, nor any powers, neither
height nor depth, nor anything else in all creation, will be able
to separate us from the love of God that is in Christ Jesus our Lord.*

ROMANS 8:38–39 NIV

God may be invisible, but He's in touch. You may not be able to see Him, but He is in control. And that includes you—your circumstances. That includes what you've just lost. That includes what you've just gained. That includes all of life—past, present, future.

CHARLES SWINDOLL

Nothing can separate you from His love, absolutely nothing…. God is enough for time, and God is enough for eternity. God is enough!

HANNAH WHITALL SMITH

Give all your worries and cares to God, for he cares about you.

1 PETER 5:7 NLT

God's Answers

God is not only the answer to a thousand needs,
He is the answer to a thousand wants. He is the
fulfillment of our chief desire in all of life. For whether
or not we've ever recognized it, what we desire
is unfailing love. Oh, God, awake our souls to see—
You are what we want, not just what we need. Yes, our
life's protection, but also our heart's affection.
Yes, our soul's salvation, but also our heart's
exhilaration. Unfailing love. A love that will not let me go!

BETH MOORE

A wise gardener plants his seeds, then has the good sense
not to dig them up every few days to see if a crop is on
the way. Likewise, we must be patient as God brings
the answers…in His own good time.

QUIN SHERRER

We shall come one day to a heaven where we shall
gratefully know that God's great refusals were sometimes
the true answers to our truest prayer.

P.T. FORSYTH

Being able to bow in prayer as the day begins or ends gives expression to the frustrations and concerns that might not otherwise be ventilated. On the other end of that prayer line is a loving heavenly Father who has promised to hear and answer our petitions.

Dr. James Dobson

God is not interested in you praying perfectly; He just wants to spend time with you and be able to speak with you and know you are listening.

Dr. Henry Cloud

The LORD has heard my plea;
the LORD will answer my prayer.

Psalm 6:9 NLT

Take Refuge

Let my soul take refuge...beneath the shadow
of Your wings: let my heart, this sea of restless waves,
find peace in You, O God.

AUGUSTINE

God stands fast as your rock, steadfast as your safeguard,
sleepless as your watcher, valiant as your champion.

CHARLES H. SPURGEON

Let all who take refuge in you rejoice;
let them sing joyful praises forever.
Spread your protection over them,
that all who love your name may be filled with joy.

PSALM 5:11 NLT

I know that He who is far outside the whole creation takes
me within Himself and hides me in His arms.... He is my
heart, He is in heaven: Both there and here
He shows Himself to me with equal glory.

SYMEON

Why would God promise a refuge unless He knew
we would need a place to hide once in a while?

NEVA COYLE

Children of the heavenly Father
Safely in His bosom gather;
Nestling bird nor star in heaven
Such a refuge e'er was given.

CAROLINA SANDELL BERG

When God has become…our refuge and our fortress,
then we can reach out to Him in the midst of a broken
world and feel at home while still on the way.

HENRI J. M. NOUWEN

The LORD is good,
a refuge in times of trouble.
He cares for those who trust in him.

NAHUM 1:7 NIV

To Know Him

He is a God who can be found. A God who can
be known. A God who wants to be close to us. That's why
He is called Immanuel, which means "God with us."
But He draws close to us as we draw close to Him.

STORMIE OMARTIAN

Once the seeking heart finds God in personal experience
there will be no problem about loving Him.
To know Him is to love Him and to know Him better
is to love Him more.

A. W. TOZER

Jesus is God spelling himself out
in language that man can understand.

S. D. GORDON

Give us, Lord: a pure heart that we may see You,
a humble heart that we may hear You,
a heart of love that we may serve You,
a heart of faith that we may live with You.

DAG HAMMARSKJÖLD

*I want you woven into a tapestry of love, in touch with everything
there is to know of God. Then you will have minds confident
and at rest, focused on Christ, God's great mystery.
All the richest treasures of wisdom and knowledge
are embedded in that mystery and nowhere else.*

COLOSSIANS 2:2–3 MSG

Made in His image, we can have real meaning,
and we can have real knowledge through
what He has communicated to us.

FRANCIS SCHAEFFER

*He made you so you could share in His creation,
could love and laugh and know Him.*

TED GRIFFEN

The Weaver

My life is but a weaving
Between my Lord and me,
I cannot choose the colors
He worketh steadily.
Oftimes He weaveth sorrow,
And I in foolish pride
Forget He sees the upper
And I, the underside.
The dark threads are as needful
In the Weaver's skillful hand
As the threads of gold and silver
In the pattern He has planned.

There are those who suffer greatly, and yet, through
the recognition that pain can be a thread in the pattern
of God's weaving, find the way to a fundamental joy.

For whatever life holds for you and your family
in the coming days, weave the unfailing fabric
of God's Word through your heart and mind.
It will hold strong, even if the rest of life unravels.

GIGI GRAHAM TCHIVIDJIAN

However things may appear to be, of all possible
circumstances—those circumstances in whose midst
I am set—these are the best that He could choose for me.
We do not know how this is true—where would faith be
if we did?—but we do know that all things that happen
are full of shining seed.

There may be times in your life when it all seems dark
and you cannot see or trace the hand of God, yet
God is working. Just as much as He works in the bright
sunlight, He works all through the night.

*The signposts of GOD are clear
and point out the right road.
The life-maps of GOD are right,
showing the way to joy.*

PSALM 19:7–8 MSG

Comforted by God

God walks with us.... He scoops us up in His arms or
simply sits with us in silent strength until we cannot avoid
the awesome recognition that yes, even now, He is here.

GLORIA GAITHER

*May our Lord Jesus Christ himself and God our Father, who loved
us and by his grace gave us eternal comfort and a wonderful hope,
comfort you and strengthen you in every good thing you do and say.*

2 THESSALONIANS 2:16—17 NLT

Only God can truly comfort; He comes alongside us
and shows us how deeply and tenderly
He feels for us in our sorrow.

Tuck [this] thought into your heart today.
Treasure it. Your Father God cares about your daily
everythings that concern you.

KAY ARTHUR

God is our merciful Father and the source of all comfort.
He comforts us in all our troubles so that we can comfort others.
When they are troubled, we will be able to give them the same
comfort God has given us.

2 CORINTHIANS 1:3–4 NIV

All [God's] glory and beauty come from within, and
there He delights to dwell. His visits there are frequent,
His conversation sweet, His comforts refreshing,
His peace passing all understanding.

THOMAS À KEMPIS

Regardless of the need, God comforts.
He is the God of all comfort! That's His specialty.

CHARLES R. SWINDOLL

I, even I, am he who comforts you.

ISAIAH 51:12 NIV

In the Silence

The soul is a temple, and God is silently building
it by night and by day. Precious thoughts
are building it; unselfish love is building it;
all-penetrating faith is building it.

HENRY WARD BEECHER

Jesus is always waiting for us in silence.
In that silence, He will listen to us; there He will speak
to our soul, and there we will hear His voice.

MOTHER TERESA

It is in silence that God is known,
and through mysteries that He declares Himself.

ROBERT H. BENSON

*God's peace...is far more wonderful than the human mind can
understand. His peace will keep your thoughts and your hearts
quiet and at rest.*

PHILIPPIANS 4:7 TLB

If we do not listen we do not come to the truth. If we do not pray we do not even get as far as listening.... Four things go together: silence, listening, prayer, truth.

HUBERT VAN ZELLER

There are times when to speak is to violate the moment... when silence represents the highest respect. The word for such times is *reverence*. The prayer for such times is "Hallowed be thy name."

MAX LUCADO

Be still, and in the quiet moments, listen to the voice of your heavenly Father. His words can renew your spirit.... No one knows you and your needs like He does.

JANET L. SMITH

*Let all that I am wait quietly before God,
for my hope is in him.*

PSALM 62:5 NLT

Treasure in Nature

If we are children of God, we have a tremendous treasure
in nature and will realize that it is holy and sacred. We
will see God reaching out to us in every wind that blows,
every sunrise and sunset, every cloud in the sky, every
flower that blooms, and every leaf that fades.

OSWALD CHAMBERS

What a wildly wonderful world, GOD!
You made it all, with Wisdom at your side,
made earth overflow with your wonderful creations.

PSALM 104:24 MSG

All this beauty exists so you and I can see His glory,
His artwork. It's like an invitation
to worship Him, to know Him.

DONALD MILLER

Above all give me grace to use these beauties of earth
without me and this eager stirring of life within me
as a means whereby my soul may rise from creature
to Creator, and from nature to nature's God.

JOHN BAILLIE

I love to think of nature as an unlimited broadcasting
station through which God speaks to us every hour,
if only we will tune in.

GEORGE WASHINGTON CARVER

Look up at all the stars in the night sky
and hear your Father saying, "I carefully set
each one in its place. Know that I love you more
than these." Sit by the lake's edge, listening to
the water lapping the shore and hear your
Father gently calling you to that place near His heart.

WENDY MOORE

The heavens declare the glory of God;
And the firmament shows His handiwork.

PSALM 19:1 NKJV

Forever Grateful

Gratitude reminds you of what you already have, of gifts easily taken for granted. These can be as small as the beauty of an almond tree in bloom or as large as the gift of your very next breath. When you recognize every good gift ultimately comes from God, you can't help but feel grateful. This deepens the pleasure of even an ordinary day, making you not only more content, but more generous with what you've received.

Whatever you do, whether in word or deed, do it all in the name of the Lord Jesus, giving thanks to God the Father through him.

COLOSSIANS 3:17 NIV

Our inner happiness depends not on what we experience but on the degree of our gratitude to God, whatever the experience.

ALBERT SCHWEITZER

Gratitude unlocks the fullness of life. It turns what
we have into enough, and more. It turns denial into
acceptance, chaos to order, confusion to clarity. It can
turn a meal into a feast, a house into a home, a stranger
into a friend. Gratitude makes sense of our past, brings
peace for today, and creates a vision for tomorrow.

MELODY BEATTIE

Gratitude bestows reverence, allowing us to encounter
everyday epiphanies, those transcendent moments of awe
that change forever how we experience life and the world.

JOHN MILTON

*Rejoice always, pray continually,
give thanks in all circumstances.*

1 THESSALONIANS 5:16–18 NIV

God's Guidance

Show me the right path, O Lord;
point out the road for me to follow.
Lead me by your truth and teach me,
for you are the God who saves me.
All day long I put my hope in you.

PSALM 25:4–6 NLT

God, who has led you safely on so far,
will lead you on to the end. Be altogether at rest
in the loving holy confidence which you ought to have
in His heavenly Providence.

FRANCIS DE SALES

Dear Lord…. When I read Your Word, peace
and contentment fill my heart…. Help me to understand
the truth that is in the Scriptures so that I will always
stand on the solid foundation it gives me. When I read
of Your laws, I see that they are good and reliable,
and when I live by them, life works.

STORMIE OMARTIAN

Great peace have those who love Your law,
And nothing causes them to stumble.

PSALM 119:165 NKJV

The God who created the vast resources of the universe
is also the inventor of the human mind.
His inspired words of encouragement guarantee us
that we can live above our circumstances.

DR. JAMES DOBSON

The Lord is able to guide. The promises cover every
imaginable situation.... Take the hand He stretches out.

ELISABETH ELLIOT

You guide me with your counsel,
leading me to a glorious destiny.

PSALM 73:24 NLT

Renewed Strength

The LORD is the everlasting God…
He gives strength to the weary
and increases the power of the weak.
Even youths grow tired and weary,
and young men stumble and fall;
but those who hope in the LORD
will renew their strength.
They will soar on wings like eagles;
they will run and not grow weary,
they will walk and not be faint.

ISAIAH 40:28—31 NIV

Those who live prayerfully are constantly ready
to receive the breath of God,
and to let their lives be renewed and expanded.

HENRI J. M. NOUWEN

Should we feel at times disheartened and discouraged,
a simple movement of heart toward God will renew our
powers. Whatever He may demand of us, He will give us
at the moment the strength and courage that we need.

FRANÇOIS FÉNELON

Be of good courage,
And He shall strengthen your heart,
*All you who hope in the L*ORD.

PSALM 31:24 NKJV

That is God's call to us—simply to be people who are
content to live close to Him and to renew the kind of life
in which the closeness is felt and experienced.

THOMAS MERTON

I can drink freely of God's power and experience
His touch of refreshment and blessing—much like
an invigorating early spring rain.

ANABEL GILLHAM

You are arrayed in holy garments,
and your strength will be renewed
each day like the morning dew.

PSALM 110:3 NLT

The Goodness of God

All that is good, all that is true, all that is beautiful,
all that is beneficent, be it great or small, be it perfect
or fragmentary, natural as well as supernatural,
moral as well as material, comes from God.

JOHN HENRY NEWMAN

Every good and perfect gift is from above,
coming down from the Father of the heavenly lights,
who does not change like shifting shadows.

JAMES 1:17 NIV

We walk without fear, full of hope
and courage and strength to do His will,
waiting for the endless good which He is always giving
as fast as He can get us able to take it in.

GEORGE MACDONALD

If you have a special need today, focus your full attention
on the goodness and greatness of your Father
rather than on the size of your need. Your need
is so small compared to His ability to meet it.

God be thanked for that good and perfect gift,
the gift unspeakable: His life, His love,
His very self in Christ Jesus.

MALTBIE D. BABCOCK

I remain confident of this:
I will see the goodness of the LORD
in the land of the living.

PSALM 27:13 NIV

The goodness of God is infinitely more wonderful
than we will ever be able to comprehend.

A. W. TOZER

Open your eyes and see—how good GOD is.
Blessed are you who run to him.

PSALM 34:8 MSG

Place of Rest

In comparison with this big world, the human heart is
only a small thing. Though the world is so large, it is
utterly unable to satisfy this tiny heart. Our ever growing
soul and its capacities can be satisfied only in the infinite
God. As water is restless until it reaches its level,
so the soul has no peace until it rests in God.

SADHU SUNDAR SINGH

*I pray that God, the source of hope, will fill you completely with joy
and peace because you trust in him. Then you will overflow with
confident hope through the power of the Holy Spirit.*

ROMANS 15:13 NLT

Love comes while we rest against our Father's chest.
Joy comes when we catch the rhythms of His heart.
Peace comes when we live in harmony with those rhythms.

KEN GIRE

God calls us…to balance our work with rest.
And even when we're at work to rest our souls in Him.
Not to be always thinking, analyzing, and planning,
but to stay our minds on Him and live in peace.

GWEN FORD FAULKENBERRY

When you feel like life has knocked the wind out of you
and you can barely put one foot in front of the other,
God kneels down to lift you up. He carries you when
you're too weary to keep forging ahead. He nourishes
your heart with soul food and eases your mind
with the sweet water of peace.

Peace is an awareness of reserves from beyond ourselves,
so that our power is not so much in us as through us.

Be still, and know that I am God.

PSALM 46:10 NKJV

Powerful Love

I pray that you, being rooted and established in love, may have power, together with all the Lord's holy people, to grasp how wide and long and high and deep is the love of Christ, and to know this love that surpasses knowledge—that you may be filled to the measure of all the fullness of God.

EPHESIANS 3:17–19 NIV

Could we with ink the ocean fill
And were the skies of parchment made,
Were every stalk on earth a quill
And every man a scribe by trade
To write the love of God above
Would drain the ocean dry,
Nor could the scroll contain the whole
Tho' stretched from sky to sky.

MEIR BEN ISAAC NEHORAI

There is no limit to God's love. It is without measure
and its depth cannot be sounded.

MOTHER TERESA

90

The God of the universe—the One who created
everything and holds it all in His hand—
created each of us in His image, to bear His likeness,
His imprint. It is only when Christ dwells within
our hearts, radiating the pure light of His love
through our humanity that we discover who we are
and what we were intended to be.

We have been in God's thought from all eternity,
and in His creative love, His attention never leaves us.

MICHAEL QUOIST

*As high as heaven is over the earth,
so strong is his love to those who fear him.*

PSALM 103:11 MSG

Mighty to Keep

God is adequate as our keeper.... Your faith will not fail
while God sustains it; you are not strong enough to fall
away while God is resolved to hold you.

J. I. PACKER

Whom have I in heaven but You?
And besides You, I desire nothing on earth.
My flesh and my heart may fail,
but God is the strength of my heart
and my portion forever....
As for me, the nearness of God is my good;
I have made the Lord GOD my refuge.

PSALM 73:25—26, 28 NASB

Life from the Center is a life of unhurried peace
and power. It is simple. It is serene....
We need not get frantic. He is at the helm.
And when our little day is done,
we lie down quietly in peace, for all is well.

THOMAS R. KELLY

God promises to keep us in the palm
of [His] hand, with or without our awareness.
God has already made a space for us,
even if we have not made a space for God.

DAVID AND BARBARA SORENSEN

God, who is our dwelling place, is also our fortress.
It can only mean one thing, and that is,
that if we will but live in our dwelling place,
we shall be perfectly safe and secure from every assault.

HANNAH WHITALL SMITH

*He who dwells in the shelter of the Most High
will abide in the shadow of the Almighty.*

PSALM 91:1 NASB

Overcoming

Christ desires to be with you in whatever crisis you may
find yourself. Call upon His name. See if He will not
do as He promised He would. He will not make your
problems go away, but He will give you the power to deal
with and overcome them…. Suffering is endurable if we
do not have to bear it alone; and the more compassionate
the Presence, the less acute the pain.

BILLY GRAHAM

*"They will fight against you but will not overcome you, for I am
with you and will rescue you," declares the LORD.*

JEREMIAH 1:19 NIV

God can take tragedy and turn it into triumph.
He routinely does this for those who love Him.

DR. JAMES DOBSON

There is the firm commitment to the triumph
of the human spirit over adversity, the certainty that
there's a God on high who may not move mountains
but will give you the strength to climb.

GENEVA SMITHERMAN

The world is full of suffering.
It is also full of the overcoming of it.

HELEN KELLER

I can do all this through him who gives me strength.

PHILIPPIANS 4:13 NIV

He did not say, "You will never have
a rough passage, you will never be over-strained,
you will never feel uncomfortable,"
but He did say, "You will never be overcome."

JULIAN OF NORWICH

*In this world you will have trouble.
But take heart! I have overcome the world.*

JOHN 16:33 NIV

Seek First

Look at the birds of the air, that they do not sow,
nor reap nor gather into barns, and yet
your heavenly Father feeds them.
Are you not worth much more than they?
And who of you by being worried can add
a single hour to his life? And why are you worried
about clothing? Observe how the lilies of the field grow;
they do not toil nor do they spin, yet I say to you
that not even Solomon in all his glory clothed himself
like one of these. But if God so clothes the grass of the field,
which is alive today and tomorrow is thrown into the furnace,
will He not much more clothe you? You of little faith!
Do not worry then, saying, "What will we eat?" or
"What will we drink?" or "What will we wear for clothing?"
For...your heavenly Father knows that you need all these things.
But seek first His kingdom and His righteousness,
and all these things will be added to you.

MATTHEW 6:26—33 NASB

There is a peace here, a serenity, even before I enter.
Just the idea of returning becomes a balm for the wounds
I've collected elsewhere. Before I can finish even one
knock, the door opens wide and I am in His presence.

BARBARA FARMER

*Keep on asking, and you will recieve what you
ask for. Keep on seeking, and you will find.
Keep on knocking, and the door will be open
to you. For everyone who asks, receives.
Everyone who seeks, finds. And to everyone
who knocks, the door will be opened.*

MATTHEW 7:7–8 NLT

Steps of Faith

In the dark dreary nights, when the storm is at its most fierce, the lighthouse burns bright so the sailors can find their way home again. In life the same light burns. This light is fueled with love, faith, and hope. And through life's most fierce storms these three burn their brightest so we also can find our way home again.

Why should we live halfway up the hill and swathed in the mists, when we might have an unclouded sky and a radiant sun over our heads if we would climb higher and walk in the light of His face?

ALEXANDER MACLAREN

Faith goes up the stairs that love has made and looks out the window which hope has opened.

CHARLES H. SPURGEON

Faith, as the Bible defines it, is present-tense action.
Faith means being sure of what we hope for…now.
It means knowing something is real, this moment,
all around you, even when you don't see it.
Great faith isn't the ability to believe long
and far into the misty future. It's simply taking God
at His word and taking the next step.

JONI EARECKSON TADA

Faith is a living, daring confidence in God's grace,
so sure and certain that a man could stake his life
on it a thousand times.

MARTIN LUTHER

*Faith is being sure of what we hope for
and certain of what we do not see.*

HEBREWS 11:1 NIV

99

Shining Promises

Our feelings do not affect God's facts.
They may blow up, like clouds, and cover the eternal
things that we do most truly believe. We may not see
the shining of the promises—but they still shine!

AMY CARMICHAEL

God is the God of promise. He keeps His word,
even when that seems impossible; even when
the circumstances seem to point to the opposite.

COLIN URQUHART

The LORD is trustworthy in all he promises
and faithful in all he does.

PSALM 145:13 NIV

Each time a rainbow appears, stretching from one end
of the sky to the other, it's God renewing His promise.
Each shade of color, each facet of light displays the
radiant spectrum of God's love—a promise that life
can be new for each one of us.

WENDY MOORE

The Lord promises to bind up the brokenhearted,
to give relief and full deliverance to those whose spirits
have been weighed down.

CHARLES R. SWINDOLL

Trust God where you cannot trace Him.
Do not try to penetrate the cloud He brings over you;
rather look to the bow that is on it.
The mystery is God's; the promise is yours.

JOHN MACDUFF

If you are seeking after God, you may be sure of this:
God is seeking you much more. He is the Lover,
and you are His beloved. He has promised Himself to you.

JOHN OF THE CROSS

Not one word has failed of all His good promise.

1 KINGS 8:56 NASB

Delight in the Lord

Delight yourself in the LORD;
And He will give you the desires of your heart.
Commit your way to the LORD,
Trust also in Him, and He will do it.
He will bring forth your righteousness as the light
And your judgment as the noonday.

PSALM 37:4–6 NASB

Open wide the windows of our spirits
and fill us full of light; open wide the door of our hearts,
that we may receive and entertain You
with all our powers of adoration.

CHRISTINA ROSSETTI

Send me your light and your faithful care,
let them lead me;
let them bring me to your holy mountain,
to the place where you dwell.
Then will I go to the altar of God,
to God, my joy and my delight.

PSALM 43:3–4 NIV

Let us give all that lies within us…to pure praise,
to pure loving adoration, and to worship from
a grateful heart—a heart that is trained to look up.

AMY CARMICHAEL

Worship the LORD in the beauty of holiness.

PSALM 29:2 NKJV

By love alone is God enjoyed; by love alone
delighted in, by love alone approached and admired.
His nature requires love.

THOMAS TRAHERNE

Our fulfillment comes in knowing God's glory,
loving Him for it, and delighting in it.

*Faith allows us to continually delight in life since
we have placed our needs in God's hands.*

JANET L. SMITH

Countless Beauties

All the world is an utterance of the Almighty.
Its countless beauties, its exquisite adaptations,
all speak to you of Him.

PHILLIPS BROOKS

As a countenance is made beautiful by
the soul's shining through it, so the world is beautiful
by the shining through it of God.

FRIEDRICH HEINRICH JACOBI

For GOD is sheer beauty, all-generous in love,
loyal always and ever.

PSALM 100:5 MSG

From the world we see, hear, and touch,
we behold inspired visions that reveal God's glory.
In the sun's light, we catch warm rays of grace
and glimpse His eternal design. In the birds' song,
we hear His voice and it reawakens our desire for Him.
At the wind's touch, we feel His Spirit and
sense our eternal existence.

Forbid that I should walk through Thy beautiful world
with unseeing eyes:
Forbid that the lure of the market-place should ever
entirely steal my heart away from the love of the
open acres and the green trees:
Forbid that under the low roof of workshop or
office or study I should ever forget
Thy great overarching sky.

JOHN BAILLIE

Our Creator would never have made such lovely days,
and given us the deep hearts to enjoy them,
above and beyond all thought, unless we were
meant to be immortal.

NATHANIEL HAWTHORNE

*May God give you eyes to see beauty
only the heart can understand.*

Your Personal God

Don't be afraid, I've redeemed you.
I've called your name. You're mine.
When you're in over your head, I'll be there with you.
When you're in rough waters, you will not go down.
When you're between a rock and a hard place,
it won't be a dead end—
Because I am GOD, your personal God,
The Holy of Israel, your Savior.
I paid a huge price for you…!
That's how much you mean to me!
That's how much I love you!

ISAIAH 43:1–4 MSG

Our days are filled with tiny golden minutes
with eternity in them. Our lives are immortal.
One thousand years from this day you will be more
alive than you are at this moment. There is a future life
with God for those who put their trust in Him.

BILLY GRAHAM

The LORD is my strength and my shield;
my heart trusts in him, and he helps me.

PSALM 28:7 NIV

God wants you to know Him as personally as He knows
you. He craves a genuine relationship with you....
People don't become best friends without talking to
each other, without spending time together.... That's
how it works with God too. He didn't make us robots,
preprogrammed to love Him and follow Him.
He gave us free will and leaves it to us to choose to spend
time with Him. That way it's genuine.
That way it's a real relationship.

TOM RICHARDS

If God be for us, who can be against us?

ROMANS 8:31 KJV

Waiting Quietly

Sit quietly in the presence of God, allowing Him to
give you the "peace which surpasses all understanding"
(Philippians 4:7). It's a peace so deep and profound that
it's unexplainable. Let it come. Let it assure you that
whatever the situation may be, it is in God's powerful
and protective hands—and so are you.

Don't fret or worry. Instead of worrying, pray.
Let petitions and praises shape your worries into prayers,
letting God know your concerns.

PHILIPPIANS 4:6 MSG

In waiting we begin to get in touch with the rhythms
of life—stillness and action, listening and decision.
They are the rhythms of God. It is in the everyday
and the commonplace that we learn patience,
acceptance, and contentment.

RICHARD J. FOSTER

God makes a promise—faith believes it,
hope anticipates it, patience quietly awaits it.

The best reason to pray is that God is really there.
In praying, our unbelief gradually starts to melt.
God moves smack into the middle of even
an ordinary day…. Prayer is a matter of keeping at it….
Thunderclaps and lightning flashes are very unlikely.
It is well to start small and quietly.

EMILY GRIFFIN

Stillness is a state of calm. Nothing brings calm like
prayer, nor will anything restore your peace like the
quietness of conversation with God. Stillness is a form of
waiting. And stillness is faith in the peace that is coming.

I wait for the LORD, my soul waits,
and in his word I put my hope.

PSALM 130:5 NIV

Pour Out Your Heart

The simple fact of being...in the presence of the Lord
and of showing Him all that I think, feel, sense,
and experience, without trying to hide anything,
must please Him. Somehow, somewhere, I know that
He loves me, even though I do not feel that love
as I can feel a human embrace, even though I do not hear
a voice as I hear human words of consolation....
God is greater than my senses, greater than my thoughts,
greater than my heart. I do believe that He touches me
in places that are unknown even to myself.

HENRI J. M. NOUWEN

Lord Jesus...
May I know You more clearly,
Love You more dearly
And follow You more nearly
Day by day. Amen.

RICHARD OF CHINCHESTER

God is like a safe house. He gives peace in the midst
of drama. He gives you space to think and regroup.
Like a house in a storm, a roof over your head and walls
around you won't stop the rain or halt the thunder,
but it sure keeps you dry in the midst of it.
Open the door and come on in.

Genuine heart-hunger, accompanied by sincere seeking
after eternal values, does not go unrewarded.

JUSTINE KNIGHT

I long, yes, I faint with longing
to enter the courts of the LORD.
With my whole being, body and soul,
I will shout joyfully to the living God.

PSALM 84:2 NLT

Pour out your heart to God your Father.
He understands you better than you do.

Always There

God is the sunshine that warms us, the rain that melts the
frost and waters the young plants. The presence of God is
a climate of strong and bracing love, always there.

JOAN ARNOLD

We need never shout across the spaces to an absent God.
He is nearer than our own soul,
closer than our most secret thoughts.

A. W. TOZER

If I go up to the heavens, you are there;
if I make my bed in the depths, you are there.
If I rise on the wings of the dawn,
if I settle on the far side of the sea,
even there your hand will guide me,
your right hand will hold me fast.

PSALM 139:7–10 NIV

God is always present in the temple of your heart…
His home. And when you come in to meet Him there,
you find that it is the one place of deep satisfaction
where every longing is met.

Always be in a state of expectancy, and see that you leave
room for God to come in as He likes.

OSWALD CHAMBERS

A living, loving God can and does make His presence
felt, can and does speak to us in the silence of our hearts,
can and does warm and caress us till we no longer doubt
that He is near, that He is here.

BRENNAN MANNING

The LORD your God is with you....
He will take great delight in you,
he will quiet you with his love,
he will rejoice over you with singing.

ZEPHANIAH 3:17 NIV

Rest in Him

Count on God's personal love for you.
He won't leave, won't walk out, won't betray.
He isn't a human capable of erratic tendencies.
His promise to stand by you is bankable. So when life
circumstances are unsettled, you can have perfect peace
because the one who steadily sustains you doesn't shift,
slip, warp, crack, disappear, or change.

Truly my soul finds rest in God;
my salvation comes from him.
Truly he is my rock and my salvation;
he is my fortress, I will never be shaken....
Trust in him at all times, you people;
pour out your hearts to him,
for God is our refuge.

PSALM 62:1–2, 8 NIV

Joy comes from knowing God loves me
and knows who I am and where I'm going...that my
future is secure as I rest in Him.

DR. JAMES DOBSON

Let the beloved of the LORD rest secure in him,
for he shields him all day long,
and the one the LORD loves rests between his shoulders.

DEUTERONOMY 33:12 NIV

Rest. Rest. Rest in God's love. The only work you
are required now to do is to give your inmost intense
attention to His still, small voice within.

MADAME JEANNE GUYON

When God finds a soul that rests in Him
and is not easily moved…to this same soul
He gives the joy of His presence.

CATHERINE OF GENOA

Rest in the LORD, and wait patiently for him.

PSALM 37:7 KJV

An Invitation

Are you tired? Worn out? Burned out on religion?
Come to me. Get away with me and you'll recover your life.
I'll show you how to take a real rest. Walk with me and work with
me—watch how I do it. Learn the unforced rhythms of grace.
I won't lay anything heavy or ill-fitting on you.
Keep company with me and you'll learn to live freely and lightly.

MATTHEW 11:28–30 MSG

[God] is looking for people who will come
in simple dependence upon His grace, and rest in simple
faith upon His greatness. At this very moment,
He's looking at you.

JACK HAYFORD

When we lay the soil of our hard lives
open to the rain of grace and let joy penetrate
our cracked and dry places, let joy soak into our broken
skin and deep crevices, *life* grows.

ANN VOSKAMP

Come, all you who are thirsty,
come to the waters;
and you who have no money,
come, buy and eat!
Come, buy wine and milk
without money and without cost.
Why spend money on what is not bread,
and your labor on what does not satisfy?
Listen, listen to me, and eat what is good,
and your soul will delight in the richest of fare.
Give ear and come to me;
hear me, that your soul may live.

ISAIAH 55:1–3 NIV

Come with me by yourselves to a quiet place
and get some rest.

MARK 6:31 NIV

River of Delights

God's love is like a river springing up in the Divine
Substance and flowing endlessly through His creation,
filling all things with life and goodness and strength.

THOMAS MERTON

Your love, O LORD, reaches to the heavens,
your faithfulness to the skies.
Your righteousness is like the mighty mountains,
your justice like the great deep....
How priceless is your unfailing love!
Both high and low among men
find refuge in the shadow of your wings.
They feast on the abundance of your house;
you give them drink from your river of delights.
For with you is the fountain of life;
in your light we see light.

PSALM 36:5–9 NIV

His overflowing love delights to make us partakers
of the bounties He graciously imparts.

HANNAH MORE

The LORD will guide you always;
he will satisfy your needs in a sun-scorched land
and will strengthen your frame.
You will be like a well-watered garden,
like a spring whose waters never fail.

ISAIAH 58:11 NIV

When the soul finds a home in the heart of God,
it has found heaven. God desires to bring that heaven to
everyone on earth. When we align ourselves to His will,
we become channels between His eternal paradise
and the world as we know it. Wading in the stream
of His grace, our banks overflow to those around us,
bringing heaven to earth.

BARBARA FARMER

What extraordinary delight we find
in the presence of God. He draws us in,
His welcome so fresh and inviting.

A Safe Journey

We are not alone on our journey.
The God of love who gave us life
sent us [His] only Son to be with us at all times
and in all places, so that we never have to feel
lost in our struggles but always can trust
that God walks with us.

HENRI J. M. NOUWEN

You have made known to me the path of life;
you will fill me with joy in your presence.

PSALM 16:11 NIV

May your life become one of glad and unending praise
to the Lord as you journey through this world.

TERESA OF ÀVILA

God has not promised us an easy journey,
but He has promised us a safe journey.

WILLIAM C. MILLER

He rescues you from hidden traps,
shields you from deadly hazards.
His huge outstretched arms protect you—
under them you're perfectly safe;
his arms fend off all harm.
Fear nothing—not wild wolves in the night,
not flying arrows in the day,
not disease that prowls through the darkness,
not disaster that erupts at high noon....
"If you'll hold on to me for dear life," says GOD,
"I'll get you out of any trouble.
I'll give you the best of care
if you'll only get to know and trust me.
Call me and I'll answer, be at your side in bad times."

PSALM 91:3–6, 14–15 MSG

It is God to whom and with whom we travel,
and while He is the End of our journey,
He is also at every stopping place.

ELISABETH ELLIOT

Made for Joy

Our hearts were made for joy. Our hearts were made
to enjoy the One who created them. Too deeply planted
to be much affected by the ups and downs of life,
this joy is a knowing and a being known by our Creator.
He sets our hearts alight with radiant joy.

WENDY MOORE

Now may the Lord of peace himself give you his peace at all times
and in every situation. The Lord be with you all.

2 THESSALONIANS 3:16 NLT

Live for today but hold your hands open to tomorrow.
Anticipate the future and its changes with joy.
There is a seed of God's love in every event,
every circumstance, every unpleasant situation
in which you may find yourself.

BARBARA JOHNSON

Joy is not happiness so much as gladness;
it is the ecstasy of eternity in a soul that has made peace
with God and is ready to do His will.

The miracle of joy is this: It happens when there is no apparent reason for it. Circumstances may call for despair. Yet something different rouses itself inside us.... We are able to remember what the sunrise looks like.... We remember God. We remember He is love. We remember He is near.

RUTH SENTER

If one is joyful, it means that one is faithfully living for God, and that nothing else counts; and if one gives joy to others one is doing God's work. With joy without and joy within, all is well.

JANET ERSKINE STUART

The joy of the LORD is your strength.

NEHEMIAH 8:10 KJV

The Gift of Grace

There is nothing but God's grace. We walk upon it;
we breathe it; we live and die by it; it makes the
nails and axles of the universe.

ROBERT LOUIS STEVENSON

The "air" which our souls need also envelops all of us
at all times and on all sides. God is round about us in
Christ on every hand, with many-sided and all-sufficient
grace. All we need to do is to open our hearts.

OLE HALLESBY

God is so rich in mercy, and he loved us so much,
that even though we were dead because of our sins,
he gave us life.... God saved you by his grace when you believed.
And you can't take credit for this; it is a gift from God.

EPHESIANS 2:4–5, 8 NLT

Jesus Christ opens wide the doors of the treasure house
of God's promises, and bids us go in and take with
boldness the riches that are ours.

CORRIE TEN BOOM

Grace is no stationary thing, it is ever becoming.
It is flowing straight out of God's heart.
Grace does nothing but re-form and convey God.
Grace makes the soul conformable to the will of God.
God, the ground of the soul, and grace go together.

MEISTER ECKHART

Grace and gratitude belong together like heaven and
earth. Grace evokes gratitude like the voice an echo.
Gratitude follows grace as thunder follows lightning.

KARL BARTH

GOD is sheer mercy and grace;
not easily angered, he's rich in love.

PSALM 103:8 MSG

God's Eternal Love

The LORD is like a father to his children,
tender and compassionate to those who fear him.
For he knows how weak we are;
he remembers we are only dust.
Our days on earth are like grass;
like wildflowers, we bloom and die.
The wind blows, and we are gone—
as though we had never been here.
But the love of the LORD remains forever....
The LORD has made the heavens his throne;
from there he rules over everything.

PSALM 103:13–17, 19 NLT

For God's love is literally infinite. It is the shoreless sea
we are destined to swim in, surf in, and grow in forever.

PETER KREEFT

The reason we can dare to risk loving others is that
"God has for Christ's sake loved us." Think of it!
We are loved eternally, totally, individually, unreservedly!
Nothing can take God's love away.

GLORIA GAITHER

Amid the ebb and flow of the passing world,
our God remains unmoved,
and His throne endures forever.

ROBERT COLEMAN

Great is his love toward us,
and the faithfulness of the LORD
endures forever.

PSALM 117:2 NIV

The crashing wave finally reaches peace as it breaks upon
the land...so our turbulent spirits find rest as we break
upon the vast shoreline of God's love.

JANET L. SMITH

I am wholly His; I am peculiarly His;
I am universally His; I am eternally His.

THOMAS BENTON BROOKS

God knows the rhythm of my spirit
and knows my heart thoughts.
He is as close as breathing.